You Can Draw
BIBLE STORIES
for Kids

Sandy Silverthorne

HARVEST HOUSE PUBLISHERS
EUGENE, OREGON

Cover by Left Coast Design, Portland, Oregon

Visit **YouCanDrawBibleStories.com** for more information, including illustrations, drawing tips, and video tutorials.

YOU CAN DRAW BIBLE STORIES FOR KIDS
Copyright © 2014 by Sandy Silverthorne
Published by Harvest House Publishers
Eugene, Oregon 97402
www.harvesthousepublishers.com

ISBN 978-0-7369-5500-3 (pbk.)
ISBN 978-0-7369-5501-0 (eBook)

SFI® Certified Sourcing
www.sfiprogram.org
SFI-00453

Printed in the United States of America

13 14 15 16 17 18 19 20 21 22 / ML-CD / 10 9 8 7 6 5 4 3 2 1

To Vicki and Christy—thanks for all your love, laughter, and support. We do have a good time.

To Mom and Dad—you always knew I could do this. Who would have thought?

And to Mrs. Eidam, my high school art teacher—you liked my cartoons even when I was just a skinny sophomore. Thanks.

Contents

Introduction:
Drawing Is Easier Than You Think!

You Can Draw Bible Stories is more than just part of the title of this book—it's a fact! Whether you're an experienced artist or you don't know which end of the pencil to use, this book helps you learn how to sketch, design, create, and illustrate some really cool pictures. And all the while you'll be learning some awesome stuff from the Old and New Testaments.

On each page you'll discover a story, such as David and Goliath, Noah and his ark, or Zacchaeus up in the tree. Then you'll get a chance to illustrate the whole thing. You'll draw the people, the animals, and even the places where these stories took place. And don't worry—you'll get step-by-step examples and even some "fill in the blanks" to help you along the way.

To get you ready to illustrate your own book, you'll need to gather your supplies. Do you like to draw with a pencil, a pen, or a crayon? Whichever you prefer, keep one or two on hand. And although you can draw right in this book if you like, you might get some extra paper as well so you can practice a few times on each drawing.

Now let's try some simple drawings to get your creative muscles warmed up. Let's start with a person. Almost everyone I know can draw a simple stick figure. So go ahead and draw one. You know, big head, stick body, arms, and legs. We'll draw a stick girl in a second.

You know, I've got to say I've never seen anyone walking around with their arms and legs sticking out like that. So for our first move, let's get the arms down to the side, the way most of us stand. And let's have the legs go down so they touch the ground.

isn't that better? Now here's a little trick using parallel lines. Parallel lines are just lines that go along with one another like this:

Parallel Lines

Now use your newfound friends—your parallel lines—and fill out the guy. Draw a line next to the stick figure lines on his body, arms, and legs. See, he's not a stick anymore. He's beginning to fill out. Like a real guy!

Look at that! You've already drawn a person and we're not even finished with the introduction yet!

You're on a roll.

I'd say we should try a girl now. Same thing—start with a stick girl. That's right, add her little triangular dress there and two sticks for legs. Now let's do the same thing with our parallel lines. Use them to make arms, legs, and her body. Add some long hair and a pretty face, and voilà! A little girl!

Faces

When you're drawing simple cartoons, facial expressions are important. How is the person feeling? Happy? Sad? Mad? Here's a secret: They're also really easy to draw. Check this out—here are some happy, sad, confused, scared, and angry faces.

Now draw some faces in the blank circles below: Try drawing someone who's happy. Now draw a sad face. How about a sleepy person? Or someone who's seasick? Add some hair and maybe glasses or a beard. We'll do some more expressions later on in the book.

Hands

I know, nobody likes to draw hands. But you can do it. It just requires a little practice. So here are a few tips that will help you out. Start by drawing a little sun. That's right. Now add five little sun rays coming out. Now add parallel lines, close them off at the ends, and there you've drawn a hand!

More...

And here's an added bonus. *You Can Draw Bible Stories* has a website! It's full of information, illustrations, trivia questions, drawing tips, and even video tutorials to help you become the best drawer...uh, *artist,* you can imagine! Just check with your parents to make sure it's okay and then go to **YouCanDrawBibleStories.com** and check it out.

But for now, just turn the page, and let's get started!

1

Adam and Eve
Genesis 1–3

In the beginning God created the heavens and the earth.
—GENESIS 1:1

In the beginning...

God created everything—the sun, the moon, all the stars, and the whole earth! He made the mountains, the oceans, and all the plants and animals. If you're God, you can pretty much do anything, so creating everything was easy for Him.

Then God created the first two people on earth. Their names were Adam and Eve.

God placed His two new kids inside a beautiful garden called Eden. (It was probably about where Iraq is now.) There were tall trees, rivers, all kinds of fruit trees from which to eat...and one fruit tree they were definitely *not* to eat from. But more on that later.

What do you think the Garden of Eden looked like? Here's my idea, but why don't you add some more trees, bushes, and maybe some animals. Make it beautiful!

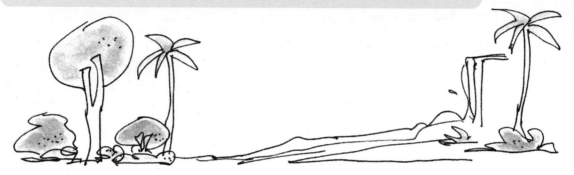

Here is a simple way to draw trees. Just draw a circle and then give it a trunk. Easy, huh?

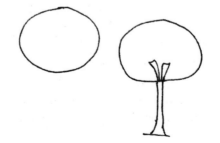

You Can Draw Bible Stories for Kids

Here's an easy way to draw a palm tree. Start by drawing a star, and then add a long trunk. You've got an instant palm tree!

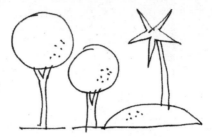

Now let's try drawing these all together. Draw a big circle, a smaller circle, a star, and a half circle. Draw their trunks, and you've got two leafy trees, a palm tree, and a bush. Easy!

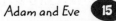

After God created Adam, He gave him an important job—He asked Adam to name all the animals He'd created. That's right, Adam came up with names like cat, dog, orangutan, and giraffe.

Can you imagine what that must have looked like? Did Adam go find every animal, or did each one come to him?

Here's Adam. Why don't you draw some animals waiting to get their names? How about a tiger, a zebra, and a skunk?

Let's draw the tiger first. Start with a circle for his head. Add two triangles for ears. Then do two eyes, a circle for his nose, and a line like this. This makes him look like a cat. The body may take some practice. Start with an oval and add four legs. Here's the fun part—the stripes and the tail! Color in the stripes, and there—you have a tiger!

Speaking of stripes, let's draw a zebra next. Using parallel lines, draw an upside-down *L* for his head. His body is just a rectangle connected to the upside-down *L*. Let the legs gently drop out of the body like this...careful that they're not too long. Add two eyes and ears, a nose, stripes, and a tail, and there's your zebra. I wonder where Adam came up with *that* name!

Keeping up our theme of stripes, let's draw a fun little creature—a skunk. Start with a kind of diamond design. That's going to be his head. Keep the bottom of the diamond open. Add ears and close the top of the diamond. Now add a couple eyes (I just use dots) and his nose. Draw a line down from the nose to give him that small animal look. His body is kind of curvy as if you were drawing a vase. Add feet and a big bushy tail (make it wider than his body). Now color in most of the body black but leave some white for stripes. You've got a skunk!

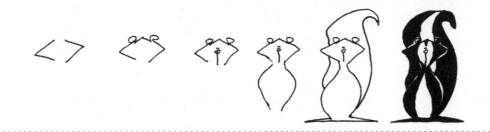

Let's draw some more of the animals Adam named that day. How about some simple ones—a cat, a dog, a bird, and a fish? To draw the cat and the dog, just start with a circle.

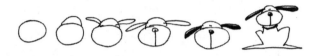

Very good! Keep practicing on your scratch sheet.

Adam and Eve had a wonderful time in the garden. It had everything they needed, and they got to be with God all the time.

But one day the snake came and tricked Eve. "Did God say you couldn't eat from every tree in the garden?"

"We can eat from all of the trees," Eve answered, "except the one over there in the middle of the garden. If we eat from that one, we'll die."

The snake replied with a lie. "You won't die! In fact, if you eat from that one, you'll be just like God! Wouldn't that be great?"

So the snake encouraged Eve to eat from the one tree that she wasn't supposed to eat from—the tree of the knowledge of good and evil. When she ate the fruit and shared it with Adam, things were never the same.

Because they rebelled against God, their friendship with Him was broken, and they were never allowed to live in the garden again. That was a dark day indeed.

But God never gave up on them. He had plans for Adam and Eve—and for all of us.

What's the Big Idea?

God created the Rocky Mountains, the Atlantic Ocean, and the Grand Canyon. But do you know what His very favorite creation is? It's you! People are the only things in the universe that God made in His own image. God calls you His special treasure (Deuteronomy 26:18). Is that cool or what?

2

Noah and the Ark

Genesis 6–9

Make yourself an ark of gopherwood.

—GENESIS 6:14 NKJV

Not long after Adam and Eve left Eden, the whole world seemed to go crazy. People started fighting, stealing, and even killing one another. God got so frustrated that He began to think He'd made a mistake by creating the earth.

"I'm going to destroy the whole thing and start over," He said. "I'm going to flood the entire earth."

But there was one man who loved God and obeyed Him in everything he did. His name was Noah. God wanted to rescue Noah from the flood that would destroy the earth. One day God spoke to him.

"Noah?"

"Yes, Lord?"

"I love you a lot."

"Thanks, Lord. I love You too."

"So tell you what, Noah...I want you to build an ark."

"A what?"

"An ark. It's a big boat. I'll show you exactly how you're to build it. You're going to need it when I flood the earth."

"Flood the *what*?"

"You'll understand in a while. The main thing is to get going and build that ark."

So Noah did exactly as the Lord instructed him. After many months, the ark was finished, and it was time to go inside.

God spoke to Noah again. "Now I want you to take two of every kind of animal into the ark with you so we won't lose any of the species that I've created."

Gathering all the animals must have been a huge chore! Can you imagine trying to round up squirrels, monkeys, hyenas, or insects? But finally it was done, and Noah, his family, and all the animals boarded the ark just before the rain started.

It rained and rained for 40 days and 40 nights until the entire earth was covered with water. But Noah, his family, and all the animals were safe inside.

The ark probably looked kind of like a barge, but when I draw it, I usually make it look like a big boat. Start with a smile. Then draw a little house on top of the smile. It's a box with a roof on top.

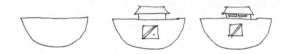

Okay, before you get too far, we need to add some animals. Let's draw an elephant. Start by making a round circle. Then add a trunk, ears, some eyes, and you've got it!

Let's add a giraffe. Draw two parallel lines for his long neck, and make his head at the top. Giraffes have little horns. And don't forget the spots!

Here's Noah beside the ark. Draw some animals going up the gangplank—how about an elephant, a zebra, a giraffe, and maybe a couple dogs and cats?

Once the rain stopped, Noah, his wife, and some of the animals came out on deck to take a look around. They gazed out over the world they once knew, but it was completely covered with water. How do you think they were feeling? Sad? Confused? Scared?

Fill in these faces to show how you think they felt.

Here's another angle of Noah's ark. But something is missing—try drawing some animals on the deck.

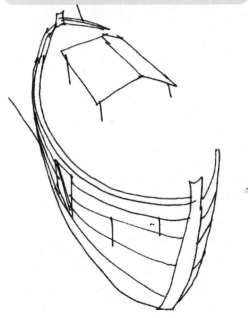

Did you know that Noah was the first person on earth to see a rainbow? It was God's way of sealing His promise that He'd never flood the entire earth again.

Now here's an easy one. Draw the rainbow Noah saw after the flood.

Have you ever been able to find the end of a rainbow? Me neither.

Color in your rainbow using all the colors you can find. What a great picture you drew! Good job!

What's the Big Idea?

God trusted Noah with a huge job—starting the human race all over again.
Whew! But God knew that Noah was obedient. After all, he'd spent years
building an ark in the middle of the desert when God told him to. God knows
that when we obey Him in the small things, He can trust us with bigger things.
What is something you can do today to show God that you want to obey Him?
Hint: How about cleaning your room or being nice to your sister? Just a thought.

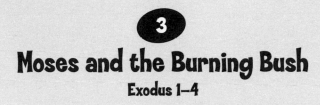

Moses and the Burning Bush

Exodus 1–4

It was by faith that Moses, when he grew up, refused to be called the son of Pharaoh's daughter. He chose to share the oppression of God's people instead.

—HEBREWS 11:24-25

Years after Noah's adventure in the ark, God planted Abraham, Isaac, and Jacob in the land of Canaan. There they flourished and multiplied. Through a series of unusual events, Jacob and his family moved to Egypt. They grew and grew until they numbered more than a million people! Pharaoh, the king of Egypt, made them slaves, forcing them to work long hours building his cities.

As Pharaoh looked out at the Israelites and saw their great numbers, he thought to himself, *If they ever rebel or go and fight for one of our enemies, we'll be toast!* (Or something like that.) So he came

JACOB'S descendants have several names. Jacob's grandfather was Abraham, and for reasons that aren't quite clear, Abraham's descendants were first known as Hebrews. Jacob himself had another name—Israel—so his descendants were also called Israel, or Israelites. One of the important tribes in this nation was named after Jacob's son Judah, so much later the entire nation also became known as Jews.

up with a plan that would limit the number of Jewish people in Egypt. He gave a command that whenever a Jewish woman gave birth to a boy, she was to throw him into the Nile River. If she gave birth to a girl, the baby was allowed to live.

When Moses' mother heard this terrible order, she didn't know what to do. She quickly wrapped her newborn son in a blanket and made a little basket boat for him. Then she set her baby boy inside and placed the basket in the Nile River. Moses' sister watched carefully from the reeds on the riverbank as the basket containing her little brother drifted down the river.

Not long after Moses was in the water, a beautiful young woman found him and took him into her house. Believe it or not, the young woman was Pharaoh's daughter! She loved the little boy that she drew out of the water. In fact, she was the one who named him Moses, which means "drawn out." She raised Moses as her own son in the palace, where he enjoyed all the food, comforts, training, and education of the royal family. But way down deep inside, Moses realized the palace wasn't his real home. God had bigger plans for him!

Let's draw Moses in the basket. Start with an oval. Then draw the side of the basket. Only draw one side because that's all we can see. Now add a blanket and Moses' face peeking out. Add some water all around his basket.

Whenever I think of Moses in his little basket in the Nile, I always picture reeds on the river-bank. They're really easy to draw—check this out. Draw as many as you'd like.

Now draw Moses' sister Miriam hiding behind the reeds on the riverbank.

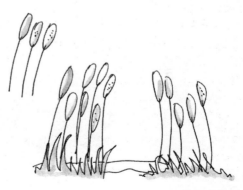

When Moses was grown up, he saw an Egyptian beating a Jewish slave. Moses got so angry that he jumped in and killed the Egyptian. Of course, this was against the law, so Moses had to run for his life. He left Egypt and lived far away in a land called Midian. Moses stayed in this desert land for 40 years, working as a shepherd.

One day while he was following the sheep near Mount Horeb, Moses saw a strange sight—a bush that was on fire! Moses knew something special was happening, so he turned aside to look.

That's when the Lord spoke to him. God spoke from the burning bush and said, "Take off your shoes, Moses, for you're standing on holy ground." Moses obeyed and took off his sandals.

Then God said, "Moses, your people in Egypt are suffering, and they're calling out to Me in their prayers."

You Can Draw Bible Stories for Kids

"Yes, Lord, I know."

"So I want to help them."

"That's great, Lord."

"And I want you to be the one to rescue them and lead them out of Egypt."

"I'm sorry…what was that?"

"I want you to get Pharaoh to let them go."

But Moses had his doubts. "Who am I that I should go and talk to Pharaoh?"

"I will be with you," answered the Lord.

"But I don't talk so well." Moses said. "Isn't there someone else you might want to send?"

"I will be with your mouth," God answered. "And I'm sending your brother Aaron to help you."

Finally Moses agreed, and back to Egypt he went.

Moses probably saw lots of bushes on fire during his years in the desert. But this one was different—it didn't burn up!

Here's the bush near Mount Horeb. Try adding the flames to make it the burning bush.

What's the Big Idea?

When God told Moses the big plans He had to save the Israelites from slavery, Moses got excited. But when God told Moses *he* was the one who needed to do it, Moses got a little nervous. "Who, me? I can't do stuff like that!" But God gave Moses the assurance that he wouldn't be alone—God would go with him.

Is anything in your life scary for you? Tell God about it. He'll help you and never make you feel foolish for asking for help. (Read James 1:5 in your Bible.)

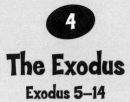

The Exodus
Exodus 5–14

When I raise my powerful hand and bring out the Israelites,
the Egyptians will know that I am the LORD.

—EXODUS 7:5

Moses and Aaron had a hard time convincing Pharaoh to let the Israelites leave Egypt. After all, the Egyptian ruler was using them as slaves, and he didn't want to lose them.

Let's try drawing Pharaoh. I always draw him with no shirt but a fancy headdress. And usually I add a cape. The Egyptians usually didn't wear robes or even shirts. And unlike the Israelite men, they shaved their beards off. Sometimes they even shaved their heads.

Let's start Pharaoh with a stick man just like we did in the introduction. Remember, we fill him out with parallel lines. Ancient Egyptians wore cloths around their waists and no shirt. That's because Egypt is usually really hot. Now give Pharaoh a face and a headdress. Put some sandals on him, and since he's the king of Egypt, give him a cape.

There—you've got Pharaoh.

You Can Draw Bible Stories for Kids

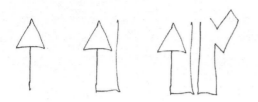

I usually draw Moses with a beard and wearing a robe. Try your own version of Moses. Start with a tall Christmas tree. Add a rectangle to it but leave the top open. Draw another rectangle right next to the first one but add another smaller rectangle coming out. Draw some fingers on each side. They're really just little circles. Give Moses a fluffy beard. Now add some detail to his robe and give him a face and a staff. Draw two feet, and you've got Moses!

Now try adding a burning bush.

God promised Moses that He'd do some pretty cool miracles to convince Pharaoh to let the people go. For example, God turned Aaron's rod into a snake. That sure got Pharaoh's attention! But then Pharaoh's magicians turned their rods into snakes too. What a mess! Read Exodus 7:8-13 to see what happened.

> Here's the royal throne room, Moses, Aaron, and Pharaoh. Add some snakes on the ground to liven things up.

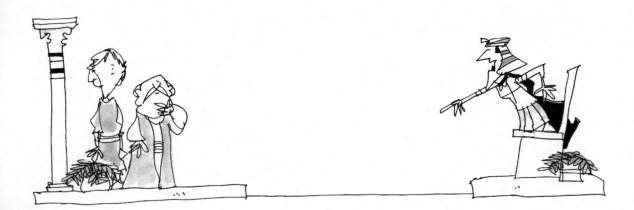

Over and over Pharaoh denied Moses' request. He refused to let the people go. Finally God showed Pharaoh He wasn't kidding. He warned the king that He was going to send ten plagues against Egypt. Surely this would convince Pharaoh to let God's people go!

 Blood. When Aaron held his staff over the Nile River, all the water turned to blood. And so did all the water in the lakes and ponds throughout Egypt.

 Frogs. Frogs were everywhere—in the houses, the bedrooms...even in the ovens!

 Gnats. There were so many of these little buggers that you could barely see the sky. Yuck.

 Flies. These flies bit people! But God's people were spared from this and the next five plagues.

 Livestock. All the livestock belonging to the Egyptians died during this plague.

 Boils. These were raised, painful bumps on all the Egyptians' skin!

 Hail. This was supernatural hail—it was mixed with fire!

 Locusts. These large grasshoppers swarmed the land and ate all the crops.

Darkness. Egyptians worshipped the sun, so this plague showed them that there was only one true God—the living God!

Passover. God warned the Jews that the firstborn child of every family in the land would die in this plague...unless the people spread the blood of the sacrificial lambs on the doorpost of their homes. The death angel would "pass over" those homes, and the firstborn children would be spared.

. . . .

Finally, after the tenth and final plague (which was also the worst!), Pharaoh gave his permission, and the Israelites were allowed to leave Egypt, leave their slavery, and leave all the heartache they'd experienced for so many years.

The nation had a great day of celebration when all the people gathered and journeyed out of Egypt.

But now what? Where was God leading them?

The people wandered in the wilderness for several days until they came to what looked like a dead end. They'd come right up against the Red Sea!

"This can't be right," they said. "Where do we go now?"

Then, to make matters worse, Pharaoh changed his mind and decided to ride out with his army and bring the people back to Egypt. Moses and the people were trapped! The Red Sea was on one side, and the Egyptian army was approaching on the other.

"Moses, where have you led us? Are you trying to kill us?"

What could they do?

Let's draw the scene. Here's Moses raising his staff over the Red Sea. Draw the waters opening up in front of him. Also add some more people if you want.

"Raise your rod over the sea and move forward," God commanded Moses.

"But, Lord—" Moses started to reply, but then he stopped. By now he'd learned to obey God even if His commands didn't seem to make sense. So Moses went forward and raised his staff over the sea.

And God did an amazing miracle—He opened up the Red Sea right in front of Moses and all the people! The water stood up like a wall on the right and on the left, leaving a path for all the people. They were able to walk through to safety on dry land!

The Exodus 41

What's the Big Idea?

Even though the people had seen God do amazing miracles in Egypt and at the Red Sea, they still had to learn to follow and obey Him. As a result, they ended up wandering in the desert for 40 years! God didn't allow them to enter the Promised Land until He knew they were ready. It's important for us to try to obey God in everything we do and even in the way we speak to one another.

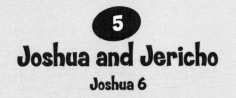

5

Joshua and Jericho
Joshua 6

The LORD said to Joshua, "I have given you Jericho,
its king, and all its strong warriors."

—JOSHUA 6:2

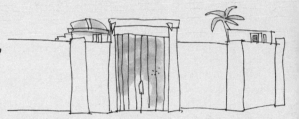

Even after all the miracles God did for His people, they constantly rebelled and disobeyed Him. As a result, after they left Egypt, they wandered around in the desert for more than 40 years! Finally the time came for them to enter the Promised Land.

Moses had died, so God raised up another leader named Joshua. One of his first assignments was to lead the people in an attack on the city of Jericho, one of the oldest and strongest cities in the world. The walls all around it were about 40 feet high! How were Joshua and his army ever going to win this battle? As usual, God had an interesting plan to defeat the city.

"Joshua?"

"Yes, Lord?"

"I've got a plan for you to defeat the city of Jericho."

"Good, 'cause it looks pretty strong to me."

"Here's what I want you to do. Have the army walk around the city once a day for six days."

"Uh-huh…"

"Then on the seventh day, have the priests blow their horns and tell the people to shout as loud as they can. I'll take care of the rest."

Joshua must have thought this was a strange strategy for attacking the city, but he obeyed God and convinced everyone to follow.

They all walked around Jericho for six days without speaking. They just walked.

I always think Jericho looked like this. Its nickname was the City of Palm Trees, so I always add them. Do you have a nickname?

Why not add some of the Jericho soldiers standing guard on top of the walls? Maybe they looked like this.

Now draw what you think Joshua's army must have looked like walking around the city.

Do you think they thought this was an odd battle plan to conquer the city?

☐ not really

☐ kind of

☐ definitely!

On the seventh day, Joshua commanded all the people to shout as loud as they could. And guess what? All the walls of Jericho came crashing down! The people of Jericho suddenly had no protection, so the Israelites easily defeated them.

Here are some of Joshua's people. Draw what you think they must have looked like when they shouted at the top of their lungs.

Even though God's plan for attacking the city was, shall we say, *unusual*, trusting and obeying Him brought the Israelites the victory!

These are some of the weapons Joshua's army used to fight the people of Jericho. On Joshua's command, the priests blew trumpets made of ram's horns. They were called shofars. The shofar was an important instrument all through Israel's history. The shofar is still blown on special occasions today.

Let's draw these.

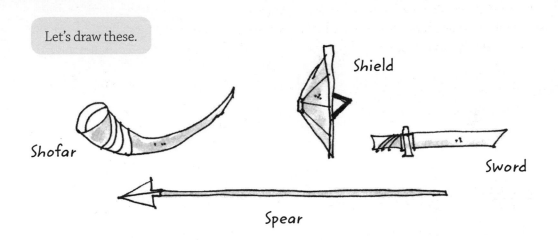

Shield

Shofar

Sword

Spear

Did You Know ?

JOSHUA (or Yeshua) is a Hebrew name. (Hebrew is the language of the Old Testament.) The Greek version is *Iesous*. (Greek is the language of the New Testament.) And the English version of *Iesous* is...you guessed it—Jesus! Joshua helped save his people, and Jesus saves us today.

What's the Big Idea?

Maybe God gave Joshua such a strange battle plan against Jericho so that when the walls fell down, everyone would know that God was the One who'd done it! Sometimes God allows hard stuff to happen in our lives so we'll get to know Him better and trust Him more.

Deborah, Barak, and Sisera
Judges 4

Deborah said to Barak, "Get ready! This is the day the LORD will give you victory over Sisera, for the LORD is marching ahead of you."
—JUDGES 4:14

The Bible introduces us to several awesome women—Ruth, Esther, Hannah, and Mary, the mother of Jesus, just to name a few. But one of the smartest and coolest women in the Old Testament was named Deborah. Her name means "bee," and she was a prophetess, speaking God's Word to the people. She was hardworking and clever, and God used her to "sting" a group of Israel's enemies.

Here's a picture of Deborah. Judges 4:5 says she judged Israel while sitting under a palm tree, so let's add that detail. If you need help drawing a palm tree, go back to chapter 1, where we learned how to draw these tropical beauties.

The captain of the other army in this story was named Sisera. His people were bad news. They harassed God's people, beat them up, and enslaved them until they couldn't take any more. The Israelites called out to God, "Save us!" and He put a plan into motion.

Try drawing Sisera. Start with a figure that looks like a saltshaker. Add lines at the top to make his helmet and a line about two-thirds of the way up the shaker. Now draw a circle (that's going to be his beard). Add a nose (it looks like a U) and two boxes sticking out for arms. Draw his eyes and lines inside the boxes for his armor. Add his belt and legs and give him a sword. Now he's ready for the battle!

You can make Sisera's soldiers look mean or angry simply by angling their eyebrows down. See? Don't they look mean?

Deborah had a friend named Barak. God had told Barak earlier to gather an army and attack Sisera, but he hadn't done it yet. Maybe he was afraid, or maybe he didn't have enough men, or maybe he didn't really believe that God was going to help him win the battle. Whatever the case, Deborah sent for Barak and encouraged him to trust God and go fight Sisera's army.

"I'll do it if you go with me," Barak answered.

"I'll go," Deborah said. "But everybody will say that Sisera was defeated by a woman."

Here's Barak. He needed Deborah's encouragement to go fight against Sisera. Give him a helmet, sword, and shield. That should help prepare him for battle.

That's odd, Barak thought. But he said okay, and off they went to Mount Tabor to face Sisera's army. Barak must have been terrified when he looked up and saw all of Sisera's men and their chariots ready for battle. But God had a plan.

Sisera thought his iron chariots would give his army the advantage over the Israelites, but they turned out to be his downfall. For just as the battle began and Sisera's chariots raced down the hill, God sent clouds and rain and flooded the valley. As a result, the chariot wheels got stuck in the mud, and the men were helpless. Deborah, Barak, and the armies of Israel defeated Sisera's men right there in the mud!

Here's Israel's camp on one side of the valley and Sisera's army on the other. Now draw the battle down in the middle by the river.

Add clouds, lightning, and rain in the sky to show how God helped the army of Israel.

After the battle Deborah's prophecy was fulfilled. Sisera escaped and hid in the tent of a woman named Jael, who was secretly an ally of Israel. When Sisera fell asleep, Jael drilled a huge tent peg right through his head! We probably won't draw that. So Deborah's word came true—Sisera was defeated by a woman.

What's the Big Idea?

God used Deborah in an amazing way. She led Israel into battle and encouraged her friend Barak to trust God and do what he was supposed to do. Barak finally became the man God had created him to be. Often God uses other people to encourage us. And He uses us to encourage others. Just ask Him to help you and keep your eyes open for someone who needs a little confidence. Who knows? You might be like Deborah to someone you know.

7
Samson and Delilah
Judges 13–16

The LORD is the strength of my life.
—PSALM 27:1 NKJV

After Deborah's victory over Sisera, the Israelites followed God for a while. But then they started straying away from Him, and that always led the tiny nation into disaster. Here was the cycle—

God's people disobey, the enemy attacks, the people cry out, God sends help.

God's people disobey, the enemy attacks, the people cry out, God sends help.

You get the idea.

During one of these cycles, a group of people called the Philistines started harassing Israel. So God called on a big guy with big potential to help out. His name was Samson. He was incredibly strong and could do amazing feats of strength, but he didn't always listen to God, and that usually led to trouble.

When Samson was born, God told his parents to set him apart for special purposes. He was to become a Nazirite—a man God would use for special assignments. Nazirites had to keep three vows—they couldn't drink wine, they could never touch anything or anyone who had died, and they could never cut their hair.

As long as Samson let his hair grow, God empowered him to have superhuman strength. One time he even defeated 1000 Philistine warriors all by himself! He was one tough dude.

Samson's troubles increased when he fell in love with a Philistine girl named Delilah. She was secretly a spy.

One night after begging and begging Samson to tell her the secret of his strength, he gave in and told her the truth. It was his hair.

"You mean to tell me if someone were to cut your hair, you'd lose all your strength?" she said, stroking his long locks.

"Yeah, if I were to cut my hair, I'd be like any other man."

So Delilah lulled Samson to sleep and shaved his head as smooth as a bowling ball. At once God's Spirit left him, and he became as weak as any other guy.

That's when the Philistines attacked Samson, tied him up, and put him in prison.

Here's Samson. Why don't you draw his really long hair? You can make it go to his shoulders, his back, or even down to his knees!

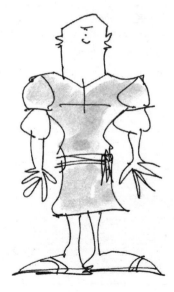

And here's Delilah. Let's draw our own version of this Philistine villain.

Start with an oval for her head. Draw two lines across the oval. Add eyes, a nose, and a little heart on the bottom line. (Those are going to be her lips.) Now draw a larger oval outside the small one. That's how I draw hair. To create Delilah's body, just draw a long box underneath her head. Now have fun drawing arms, hands, and her jewelry. Don't forget to add the scissors. She'll need those to cut Samson's hair!

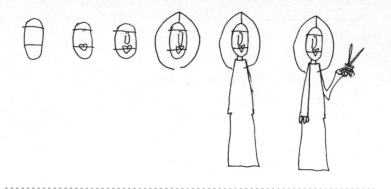

After the Philistines had kept Samson in prison for a long time, they brought him to a huge feast so they could make fun of him. They chained him between two pillars.

But...they didn't realize Samson's hair was starting to grow back.

As they laughed and pointed at him, Samson prayed to God one more time. "Lord, let me have revenge on these Philistines!"

Samson gathered all his strength and pushed against the two pillars. As he did, the pillars gave way, and the entire building collapsed, killing everyone inside, including Samson. It was Samson's final victory over the Philistines.

Samson's final act of strength occurred during the Philistines' banquet. Draw Samson in the middle pushing against the pillars. Add more Philistines if you'd like.

Samson and Delilah

What's the Big Idea?

God gives us second chances.

Samson's story is sad, but all through his life (even when he made dumb choices), one thing remained clear—God never gave up on him.

Have you ever done something you regretted? Have you ever done or said something that hurt someone else? Yeah, me too.

Aren't you glad that even when we do things that hurt others or ourselves, we can tell God we're sorry, and He will always forgive us and give us another chance?

First John 1:9 says that if we confess our sins (the bad things we do), God is faithful to forgive us and to cleanse us from all those things. Aren't you glad about that? Samson sure was.

8

David and Goliath
1 Samuel 17

The LORD rescues his people, but not with sword and spear. This is the LORD's battle.

—1 SAMUEL 17:47

As the years went by, Israel decided they wanted to be like all the other nations—they wanted a king.

They selected a tall and handsome guy named Saul. He started out well but soon strayed from following God. And to add to his problems, the Philistines (remember them from Samson's story?) kept creeping into Israel and starting fights.

One time the Philistines actually snuck right into the heart of Israel to a place called the Valley of Elah. Saul's army camped on one side of the valley, and the Philistines camped on the other.

For 40 days and 40 nights, the Philistines' champion, a giant of a guy named Goliath, made fun of Saul's men.

"Hey, you cowards, send one of your men out here to fight me! If he wins, we'll be your servants. If I win...well, you can figure it out!"

Nobody wanted to fight this guy—not even King Saul. Even from where they stood, they could tell he had to be about ten feet tall. He had body armor and weapons that Israel's army had never even heard of. And his attitude! He yelled, spat, cursed, and ridiculed Saul's men day and night for more than a month. All of Israel's soldiers were shaking in their sandals! He looks pretty tough doesn't he?

Here's Goliath without all his stuff. Take a moment and add body armor, a helmet, a spear, and a javelin. First Samuel 17:6 also mentions that he had bronze armor on his legs, so make sure you add that too.

So when David (who might have been as young as 12 at the time) showed up, he knew something was wrong. Instead of gearing up for a fight, Israel's army was cowering behind tents, trees, and each other just to get away from this Philistine bully.

Let's practice drawing some scared faces. Here are a few examples of how people look when they're scared.

Mildly Nervous

Pretty Scared

Terrified

Draw some scared faces on Saul's men as they hide from Goliath.

Who's this foreigner who dares to defy the armies of God?" David asked. "I'll take him on!"

King Saul tried to talk David out of it, but David insisted on fighting the giant.

"Well, at least wear my armor," Saul said. "That will give you some protection."

David tried it on, but it was way too big and clunky.

"It'll just get in the way," David said. "Besides, the battle is God's, not mine."

Saul wanted David to wear his armor, but it didn't fit. Draw Saul's armor on the young shepherd boy. Here's a sample of what he might have tried on.

David held out his little leather sling for Saul to see. "I hit a lion and a bear with this slingshot. With God's help, I can surely get rid of this guy."

After David left King Saul, he made his way down to the little stream that ran through the campsite. He reached into the icy water and grabbed five smooth stones.

Perfect, he thought as he shoved them into his little shepherd's bag. *These should do the trick.*

David got his five stones out of this stream. Draw them in the water. You could draw David looking for them too.

David and Goliath **65**

When the Philistine giant saw David running toward him on the battlefield, he laughed.

"This will be too easy," he snarled as he moved toward the brave young boy. He started shouting insults again, telling David his body was about to get fed to the wild animals and vultures. But David didn't listen.

David said, "Not so, big guy!" (or something like that). "God doesn't need a sword or a spear to win this battle! You're going to be delivered into our hands!"

As David continued running toward the giant, he slid his hand into his pouch. He grabbed a stone and stuck it in his leather sling. Then he swung it around his head, and at just the right time, he let go. The stone flew through the air and struck Goliath right in the forehead! Goliath went down and never got up again.

God had defeated the giant, and he used a young shepherd boy to do it. That shepherd boy eventually grew up to be the next king of Israel!

Here's the scene in the Valley of Elah. Israel's camp is on the right side, and the Philistines are on the left. Add as many soldiers as you want, but make sure you draw David and Goliath down there in the middle. Draw David's sling too.

What's the Big Idea?

The giants in our lives aren't ten-feet-tall warriors. They can be things like fear, loneliness, or troubles at home or at school. Did you know that God knows all about those giants and that they don't scare Him one bit? Just like David, you can remember that you're one of God's kids and that He's going to take care of you regardless of the giants you might face!

9
Elijah and Elisha
2 Kings 6:8-23

Elisha prayed, "O LORD, open his eyes and let him see!"
—2 KINGS 6:17

elijah elisha

Elijah and Elisha were two of the most famous prophets in the Old Testament. It's easy to get them mixed up, partly because their names are a lot alike and partly because Elijah was Elisha's mentor, or teacher. To make things even more confusing, Elijah and Elisha performed several similar miracles. They both fed people who were starving, and they both brought folks back from the dead.

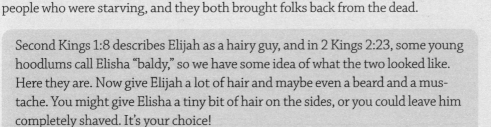

Second Kings 1:8 describes Elijah as a hairy guy, and in 2 Kings 2:23, some young hoodlums call Elisha "baldy," so we have some idea of what the two looked like. Here they are. Now give Elijah a lot of hair and maybe even a beard and a mustache. You might give Elisha a tiny bit of hair on the sides, or you could leave him completely shaved. It's your choice!

This story has to do with Elisha.

One day the king of Aram (or Syria), a bitter enemy of Israel, got so mad at Elisha that he sent an entire army to his house in Israel to capture him.

When Elisha's servant awoke that morning, he got quite a shock! As far as the eye could see, Aramean soldiers covered the landscape. And they weren't happy. The servant knew they were coming for his master, Elisha.

Let's draw Elisha's servant as he first spotted the Aramean soldiers surrounding his city. How do you think he was feeling? Nervous? Scared? Terrified? Try using some of the ideas we used in David's story (page 63) to draw people who were afraid.

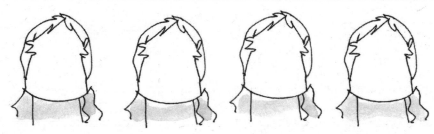

"Elisha...uh, could you come out here? There's something... well, you might want to see this," the servant stuttered.

Wow!" Elisha said as he came to the door.

"I know, there's got to be five thousand of them!"

"I'd say there's more than that," the wise prophet said.

"Oh, great. You're not helping, sir."

"Oh," Elisha said, waving his hand at the enemy army. "You mean *those* guys. I'm talking about the army of God. They've come to help us."

"When will they get here?" the servant asked nervously.

"They're here already," Elisha said. Then he prayed, "Lord, open up my servant's eyes so he can see what I see."

Instantly the servant's eyes were opened, and he could see tens of thousands of angels in chariots of fire surrounding the Aramean army.

"Feeling better now?" Elisha asked.

"Much," the servant said.

Elisha prayed again, and all the Arameans were struck with blindness. Elisha approached the leader and said, "Are you looking for Elisha the prophet? Come with me—I'll take you right to him."

But instead, Elisha led the Aramean army smack-dab into the middle of Samaria, the capital city of Israel. Then Elisha prayed again, and the Arameans got their sight back—and saw that they were completely surrounded by Israelites!

"Should we kill them?" the king of Israel asked Elisha.

"Of course not. Treat them like guests—feed them and then send them back to where they came from."

Draw an Aramean soldier. Start with a saltshaker again. Only this one has a circle on the side. That's going to be his shield. Add some lines up on top for the helmet and a *U* for his nose. Add his right arm and a couple of feet. Draw a mustache, goatee, or beard. Make the guy look really mean and scary. Remember how Elisha's servant felt when he saw them!

Here are the hills surrounding Elisha's house.

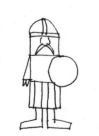

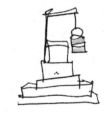

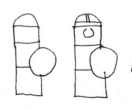

Behind them, up on the hills, draw God's army in chariots of fire. Start with a simple shape and a circle—that's going to be the chariot. To the right draw an oval—that's the horse. To make the horse's head, draw an upside down *L*. Add four legs. Now add the angel inside the chariot. And now decorate! Give your angel some wings, add a mane to the horse, and don't forget the flames. Remember, these are chariots of fire! You can draw flames just like you did on page 33.

What's the Big Idea?

Sometimes having faith means seeing things the way God does. Elisha's servant learned that lesson big-time! When God opened his eyes, the servant could see that God had sent help.

When you're facing a hard situation, ask God to help you see a little of what He's up to. He promises never to leave us, and He's always up to something that will be good for us. (Read Joshua 1:5 in your Bible.) Maybe He'll even send an army of chariots to help you out!

10

Daniel's Night with the Lions
Daniel 6

*My God sent his angel to shut the lions' mouths
so that they would not hurt me.*
—DANIEL 6:22

Daniel was probably just a teenager when the Babylonians marched into Israel, tore down Jerusalem's walls, burned the city, killed thousands of people, and took the rest captive. Daniel and many of his young friends were captured and taken from their homeland to the distant Babylonian kingdom. These young men had never seen any place like it. The city was huge and crammed full of people who never talked about the living God.

As the years in captivity went by, Daniel became so wise and popular that he was chosen to serve as one of the king's chief advisers. At that time, the king's name was Darius.

Here's a simple way to draw the king. Try it yourself!

But even in this foreign land, Daniel stayed true to the God of Israel. He prayed and worshipped God every chance he could, even when it was unpopular or even dangerous.

The king loved Daniel and respected his wisdom, knowledge, and skill in everything he did. In fact, some of the king's other advisers were jealous of Daniel. So when Darius promoted Daniel instead of his other advisers, they weren't so happy.

"We've got to do something about Daniel. He's making us look bad!"

"But what can we do? He never does anything wrong!"

"Well, he's always praying and worshipping the God of Israel. Maybe we can talk Darius into making that illegal."

"Good idea," they chuckled.

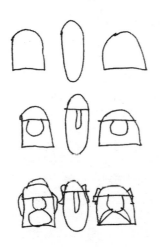

Let's try drawing the bad guys in this story. Start out your drawing with three shapes. You might make a square, circle, or oval. I did a couple of half ovals.

Draw a line across the shape about a third of the way down from the top. These are going to be their angry eyebrows. Make noses by simply drawing U shapes. Now you can get creative. Draw a goatee with a circle or a mustache with simple lines coming out from the nose. Add some hair sticking out on the sides of their heads. Add some funny hats.

Practice a few times and then draw these guys' heads on top of their bodies. There—instant bad guys!

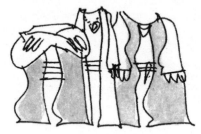

That day they went to the king and had him sign an edict stating that anyone who prayed to anybody but the king would get tossed into the lions' den.

When Daniel heard the new official order, he did what he always did—he went to his house, opened the windows toward Jerusalem, and prayed to God.

This was just what the other officials were waiting for. They quickly arrested Daniel. That night the king sadly ordered his palace guard to toss Daniel into the lions' den.

Back then, a lions' den was probably just a big hole in the ground with walls all around it. It might not even have had a roof.

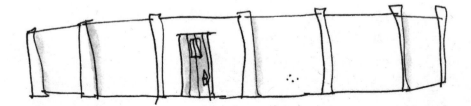

Draw what you think the lions' den looked like. Add a few lions. If you need help, here's an easy way to draw these feisty, ferocious felines.

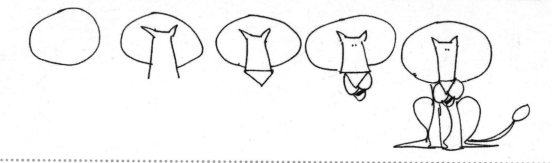

Now draw some lions in the scene with Daniel.

Because of his love for Daniel, King Darius couldn't sleep a wink all night. Early in the morning, he rushed to the lions' den.

"Daniel, are you all right? Did your God save you?"

"I'm okay, Your Highness," Daniel replied. "The Lord sent an angel, who kept the lions' mouths closed all night long!"

Because of Daniel's trust and obedience, God saved him and honored him.

Draw Daniel, his lion friends, and the king celebrating God's miraculous rescue of Daniel.

What's the Big Idea?

Even when Daniel faced lots of trouble, he stood firm and loved God with all his heart. Sometimes it's hard to tell people you love God, but every time we do it, God honors us and blesses us.

11
Esther and Mordecai
Esther 1–10

Who knows if perhaps you were made queen for just such a time as this?
—ESTHER 4:14

"Who, me?" Esther couldn't believe that her cousin Mordecai would even suggest the idea.

"Of course!" he said. "Who else?"

Mordecai had raised Esther ever since her parents had died. He was like a father to her, so she trusted and obeyed him. But this seemed impossible. How could a young Jewish girl save her entire nation?

She thought back to the day a group of officials representing Xerxes, king of Persia, had come to her home. They had come to take Esther to the palace. King Xerxes had needed a new queen, so beautiful young girls from all over the kingdom were being brought before him.

After King Xerxes had met them all, he would make his final decision, and a new queen would be crowned.

Esther had gone with them and entered the palace. She joined many other women who were being considered.

After a year, King Xerxes had made the big announcement. Esther was his new queen!

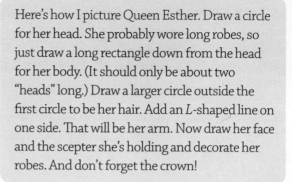

Here's how I picture Queen Esther. Draw a circle for her head. She probably wore long robes, so just draw a long rectangle down from the head for her body. (It should only be about two "heads" long.) Draw a larger circle outside the first circle to be her hair. Add an L-shaped line on one side. That will be her arm. Now draw her face and the scepter she's holding and decorate her robes. And don't forget the crown!

Draw Queen Esther

Esther and Mordecai stayed in close contact with each other after she became queen. Mordecai even camped right outside the palace so he could help Esther if she ever needed him.

One day, Haman, one of the king's advisers, had walked by the palace entrance. As was the custom, everyone bowed to honor him. Everyone except Mordecai, that is. Being a devout Jewish man, Mordecai would only bow to one—the living God. This had made Haman so mad that he wrote an order that would destroy not only Mordecai but all of his people, the Jews. In just a few months, the citizens of Persia were to attack the Jews wherever they lived. And the Jewish people could do nothing about it.

Haman was one of the worst bad guys in the entire Bible. Let's draw him here. Start with an egg-shaped oval for his head. Draw a line across the oval and add a little *U* for his nose. Under the nose draw a small circle for his beard. Add eyes and an angry mouth.

For his body, just draw a rectangle about two heads tall—that's his robe. Now add some hair, decorate his robe, and you've got Haman. Boo, hiss!

Queen Esther hadn't heard about Haman's evil plot, but now Mordecai was informing her about the situation and asking her to go to the king and plead with him to stop it.

Draw Haman

"But what can I do?" she said, "No one is allowed to go in to see the king without an invitation. If I just barge in, he *might* hold out his scepter, which would mean he's willing to see me. On the other hand, he might not, which would mean my death!"

"Don't you see?" Mordecai said. "This is the whole reason God made you queen. It was for this very time!"

"All right," Esther said. "Tell our people to pray for me, and I'll go see the king. If I die, I die. But maybe God will stop Haman's evil plan."

mordecai

Try drawing Mordecai. He was a good man who loved Esther as if she were his own daughter. Start with a shape that looks kind of like a plump rocket ship. On the sides, complete the lines that will be his arms hanging down. Draw a rounded line from shoulder to shoulder—that's his head. Now draw a friendly face and add some more detail to his robes. Add his hands, ears, and some hair, and there—you've got Mordecai!

Queen Esther's hand must have been trembling when she reached out to open the door into the king's presence. She stood in the doorway until he noticed her. When he did, a broad smile came across his face, and he held out his scepter.

"Come in, Esther." Esther was relieved when the king welcomed her into his presence.

"What can I do for you?" the king asked. "What is your request?"

"Tell you what. Why don't you let me prepare a banquet for you tomorrow, and I'll tell you then."

"Sounds wonderful."

Here's a picture of King Xerxes. How many people do you know whose name starts with an *X*?

The king was sitting on his throne when Queen Esther approached him. Thrones are easy to draw. They're really just a bunch of rectangles. Draw one big rectangle with two smaller ones on the sides. Draw some boxes here. And a box inside the original rectangle. I usually put a crown up on top so people know it's a throne. When you're feeling confident, try drawing your throne around King Xerxes above.

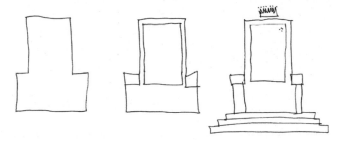

Esther and Mordecai

The next day Queen Esther prepared a huge banquet for the king. And she even invited Haman as part of her plan.

"So tell us, Queen Esther, what is your request?" the king asked.

Esther smiled and said, "I'll tell you if you both come to another banquet tomorrow night."

The next day the king and Haman once again came to a banquet Esther had prepared. After dinner, Esther rose from her place and said, "O Your Majesty, I want to let you know my request."

"What is it, my dear queen?"

"Dear husband, a plan has been hatched to destroy all of my people, here and across all the Persian empire!"

"That's horrible," the king said. "Who came up with such a plan?"

"This man!" Esther said, pointing at Haman. "It's all his idea!"

The king was so angry by this news that he ordered Haman hanged immediately.

Then he told his messengers, "Write a new edict, declaring that the Jewish people can defend themselves and be protected. Send it throughout the entire kingdom."

The king's messengers spread the news, and all the Jewish people were saved from Haman's destructive plot.

Mordecai's plan and Queen Esther's courage saved the Jewish people!

Queen Esther prepared two delicious banquets. If you had a banquet, what would you serve? Draw some of your favorite foods on the plates Esther set. Don't forget the pizza, cupcakes, and ice cream!

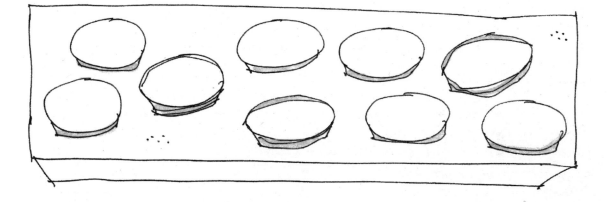

What's the Big Idea?

Do you think God was surprised when Esther became queen during this extremely difficult time in Israel's history? Not at all. In fact, He planned the whole thing! He knew Esther would be in the right place at the right time to help save her people. You know what? Sometime God might put you right where He wants you in order to be a blessing to someone else.

12

Jonah and the Big Fish
Jonah 1–3

The LORD had arranged for a great fish to swallow Jonah. And Jonah was inside the fish for three days and three nights.

—JONAH 1:17

Being a prophet for God wasn't easy, especially for Jonah. Most of the prophets got to travel around Israel and tell the people to follow God. But not him. No, not Jonah. God spoke to him one day and told him to leave his homeland and go to Nineveh, the capital of the mighty Assyrian Empire.

Nineveh—that's the worst city in the world! And none of God's people even live there—it's full of bloodthirsty Assyrians! No way, thought Jonah. *No way I'm going to Nineveh. I hate those guys!*

So instead of heading east toward Nineveh, Jonah headed west to catch a boat across the Mediterranean Sea.

"Where to?" the clerk asked.

"Anywhere but Nineveh," Jonah replied.

"Oh, you want the three o'clock ship." He handed Jonah his ticket. It read, "Anywhere but Nineveh."

Jonah paid the clerk, boarded the ship, and then went below the main deck to his room so he could take a nap. As the little vessel made its way out into the middle of the sea, disaster struck! A huge storm threatened to sink the ship and all its passengers! The sailors didn't know that God sent the storm to get Jonah's attention.

The captain rushed down and woke up the sleeping prophet.

"Get up and pray!" he shouted. "The ship's about to sink!" As Jonah came up from his quarters and out onto the deck, he realized that the storm had struck because of him.

"This is my fault," he admitted to the sailors. "If you throw me overboard, the storm will stop." After some coaxing, they finally agreed and tossed the prophet overboard. Sure enough, as soon as Jonah hit the water, the storm stopped as quickly as it had started. But what became of Jonah? Surely he couldn't last very long in the middle of the ocean.

Let's draw this exciting scene. Here are the sailors tossing Jonah overboard. You add the waves, storm clouds, rain, and lightning. Draw some of the cargo they threw over the side. Add some fish and maybe some more sailors.

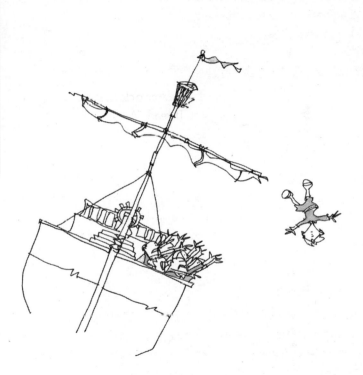

Jonah and the Big Fish

As Jonah struggled to stay afloat, he spotted a huge gray shadow coming right at him. What was it? Before he could figure it out, he saw two big eyes and a huge mouth opening wide around him.

Gulp!

Jonah was inside a huge fish! It had to be dark and very smelly. And Jonah was sure he was a goner.

Let's draw the fish. It really could look like anything, but usually I draw it to look like a whale. Start by drawing a long C. Then add the tail, his mouth, and a couple eyes. If you want to get fancy, stick a triangle-shaped fin on the side.

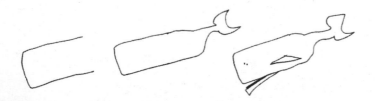

Meanwhile, inside the fish, Jonah finally came to his senses and asked God for forgiveness.

"I'm sorry, Lord. I'll go to Nineveh," he said. "I'll go wherever You want."

And he meant it.

What do you suppose it was like inside that big old fish? Draw some of the things Jonah might have found in there…maybe some small fish and some seaweed. How about a tire, some birthday cake, and an old bicycle? You never know.

Jonah and the Big Fish

After Jonah prayed, God told the fish to spit Jonah out on the dry land. Yuck.

Jonah had learned his lesson. He journeyed straight to Nineveh and preached to the people of that evil Assyrian city. And believe it or not, all the people turned from their evil ways and decided to follow God! Makes you wonder...if Jonah had gone there in the first place, would he have saved himself a lot of grief? He definitely would have smelled better.

Nineveh was a huge walled city with a bunch of mean, unruly people inside.

Draw some unruly guys sitting on the walls and hanging around the town. I draw unruly guys with angry looks on their faces. (Remember the mean eyebrows?) And try making their teeth look really mean.

Start with a circle. Then draw three lines across the circle. Add a couple dots for eyes (or draw them however you want). Now, for their teeth, just add a line in the middle and a bunch of vertical (that means up and down) lines. They're looking mean and unruly already, aren't they? Add a nose, some unruly hair, a spear, and you've got it.

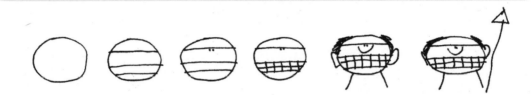

What's the Big Idea?

Jonah learned it's good to obey God the first time. That way, you won't end up smelling like the inside of a fish.

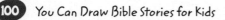

13

Mary, Joseph, and Jesus
Matthew 2:1–12; Luke 2

Look! The virgin will conceive a child! She will give birth to a son, and they will call him Immanuel, which means "God is with us."

—MATTHEW 1:23

We usually talk about Jesus' birth at Christmas, but the story is so cool, why not celebrate it any time of the year?

One day, an angel appeared at Mary's house in Nazareth and told her she was going to give birth to a very special child. He was going to be God's Son! Mary told her fiancé, Joseph, about the angel's visit, and they were both amazed and a little confused.

Several months later, the young couple heard that the Roman government was taking a census and requiring everybody to leave their homes and go back to where their ancestors had come from. Rome wanted to count all the people, and everyone had to obey.

So Mary and Joseph packed up and walked the 80 miles to Bethlehem, the town where Joseph's ancestors had lived. They crossed streams and rivers and had to be constantly alert for robbers or wild animals. But finally they reached their destination—and just in time!

After the long journey, Mary just wanted to lie down on a warm bed, but it was not to be. Every extra room in the little town was already filled with guests, so Mary and Joseph ended up sleeping behind someone's house in a little cave that was being used as a stable.

Hours later, in the middle of that dark, cold night, Jesus was born! As Mary looked into her little boy's eyes, she forgot the pain and trouble she had endured to get there. She felt nothing but love and awe for her little baby boy.

But was it true? Was this really God's Son she was holding in her arms? The visit from the angel seemed like a lifetime ago to the young Hebrew girl. As she wondered about all this in her heart, a wonderful thing happened. Some shepherds from the nearby fields arrived with tales of angels and singing and great news for everybody. They said the baby in the feeding trough was going to be the Savior of the world!

Did You Know

?

BETHLEHEM means "house of bread." It was the home of David and his family. Joseph was a descendant of David, so he and Mary had to go there to register for the census.

This must have encouraged Mary and Joseph as they stood in that drafty stable with their newborn child. Here are a couple of shepherds. Let's learn how to draw some sheep around them.

When you draw a sheep, start with an oval. Then add a head and four lines for feet. Fill in those lines and add the tail. See how easy it is?

This is the stable where Mary, Joseph, and Jesus stayed that first night in Bethlehem. Draw Mary and Joseph and show the infant Jesus in the manger.

The manger was just a little box where the animal food was kept. It's easy to draw. Start with a rectangle. Then draw what looks like a roof on it. Draw a line up near the top of the "roof." Then make a few lines across the box. Those are the little cloths that Jesus was wrapped in. Now draw two eyes and a little hair to show the baby Jesus peeking out. Draw an X on the bottom of the box, fill it in with parallel lines, and you've got the manger.

Let's learn how to draw some of the animals that might have been there that night. No, not zebras, lions, or wolves. How about a couple cows, some sheep, and a goat?

Cows are fun to draw. You can start with a big oval like this for their body. Draw four legs. Use a big *8* for the head. Add horns, ears, eyes, and a nose.

You Can Draw Bible Stories for Kids

Goats are like big dogs with horns and a little beard.

Now draw some animals in the stable.

Sometime later, some wise men showed up to worship the baby Jesus. The Bible never says how many wise men there were, but we'll go with tradition and say there were three.

Let's try drawing these visitors from the East. It's easy. Start with a circle for the head. Then add a fancy hat or crown. Draw a cone for their body and a sideways triangle for their arm. Add a face and a gift for the baby Jesus. What is it? Gold, frankincense, or myrrh?

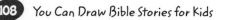

Draw the wise men

Fun Idea

Why not use one or more of your drawings as the front of a personal Christmas card for someone you know? Get some construction paper or card stock and fold it in half.

You can use the wise men or the manger scene. Create a drawing on the front and write "Merry Christmas" on the inside.

Don't forget to sign your name!

What's the Big Idea?

God brought the shepherds and wise men to Mary and Joseph. In the same way, He often brings people into our lives to remind us how much He loves us and to tell us that He's up to something special in our lives.

Has anyone ever helped you to feel special?

14
John the Baptist
Mark 1:1-11

I baptize you with water; but someone is coming soon who is greater than I am.
—LUKE 3:16

Did you know that Jesus had a cousin? His name was John, but most people today refer to him as John the Baptist. He was a passionate evangelist who lived in the desert by the Jordan River. John baptized people, but he was also a powerful preacher. He'd say things like this: "Don't just get baptized and *say* you follow God to look good in front of other people. Let's see a real change in your life too."

One day something happened that John would remember for the rest of his life. As he was in the river baptizing, Jesus stepped out of the crowd and said, "I want you to baptize Me."

John tried to talk Jesus out of it. "I should be getting baptized by You!"

But Jesus said, "No, let's do this. It's important."

So John agreed, and the two of them made their way out to the middle of the river, where John eased Jesus down into the water. And as soon as Jesus came up, the heavens were opened, and the Holy Spirit came down on Jesus just as a bird would land on a branch. At the same time, a voice came from heaven saying, "This is My beloved Son. I'm really happy with Him."

So John witnessed God the Father (the voice from heaven), God the Son (Jesus), and God the Holy Spirit (who came down like a bird) all together in one place. What an amazing day!

Matthew 3:1-4 tells us several things about John.

- He lived out in the desert (or wilderness).

- He wore a coat made of camel hair and a leather belt.

  - His diet was mostly locusts, which are kind of like grasshoppers (yuck!), and honey (yum!).

Did You Know

IN JOHN'S DAY people got baptized to show they were turning away from their sins. Nowadays, people get baptized to let people know that they're forgiven and that they want to follow Jesus. Water baptism is a great way to start your new life with Jesus.

Let's draw all this stuff. Here's a simple way to draw a locust. Start with a sideways ice cream cone. Then add his eyes and legs. Give him antennae on the top of his head, and you've got a locust!

And here's a simple way to draw a beehive. It's like an upside-down *U*. Draw some lines across it and then add some bees buzzing around. Do you like honey?

The Jordan River is the eastern border of modern-day Israel. That's where John did his baptizing. Draw John and Jesus out in the water. Now draw the dove flying down to Jesus and add God's words, "This is My beloved Son."

This is a simple dove you can draw for this scene.

John the Baptist

What's the Big Idea?

John the Baptist was a humble servant of God. He knew he had an assignment—to prepare the way for Jesus, the Son of God, and to let people know that He was coming. He also challenged people to really follow God, not just talk about it.

What's something you can do today to follow Jesus? Could you pray for someone who needs help? Maybe you could be nice to the new kid in school or help your mom or dad with something without being asked. There are lots of ways to show that you're a follower of Jesus!

15
Feeding the 5000
John 6:1–15

There's a young boy here with five barley loaves and two fish. But what good is that with this huge crowd?

—JOHN 6:9

Jesus stood on the sunny hillside and talked about God's love to thousands of people who had gathered there. It was a wonderful afternoon, and after several hours, Philip, one of Jesus' disciples, came to Him.

"This has been great," he said. "The people are having a good time."

Jesus looked up and said, "How are we going to buy enough bread to give all of them lunch?"

"We? As in...us?" Philip asked. "Even if we had a year's salary, we couldn't afford enough food to feed all these people!"

Just then Andrew came up. "A kid here has five loaves of bread and a couple fish...but that's probably not enough to feed all these people, is it?"

Jesus looked around. "Have the people sit down."

The disciples had everyone sit in small groups. The crowd covered the entire hillside, and in their white and tan robes, they looked like little sheep on the grassy slope.

Jesus took the small basket from the little boy, thanked His heavenly Father, and had the disciples gather around. Jesus started pulling bread and fish out of the basket and handing them to His disciples. "Start giving these to everyone," He said.

Here's the basket the little boy gave to Jesus. Draw five loaves of bread and two fish inside.

Pretty soon, Jesus' disciples (and maybe even the little boy) were wandering around the crowd like waiters, handing out fish and bread to all the hungry people.

Here's Jesus. Draw more of the fish and the bread He's handing out.

After a while, everyone sat back in the sun and sighed. They were all so full that it felt like Thanksgiving.

"That was delicious! I'm stuffed!"

"Don't let anything go to waste," Jesus instructed the disciples.

Here's your lunch box. Draw what you'd like to be inside it.

They found some empty baskets and collected the leftovers—12 baskets full! Enough for every one of the 12 disciples!

Try drawing that generous little boy. He gave his whole lunch to Jesus. Would you have done that?

He's fun to draw. Start by drawing a funny little *H*. Make sure the crossbar is curved. Now draw parallel lines next to your *H* to make a couple little arms. Put little triangles on top of the arms. Now draw a face on the boy and add some hair.

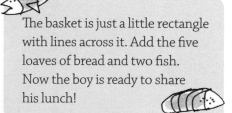

The basket is just a little rectangle with lines across it. Add the five loaves of bread and two fish. Now the boy is ready to share his lunch!

This is the hillside where Jesus was feeding everybody. Add the disciples and the people. (You don't have to draw all 5000.)

Just for fun, draw the 12 baskets that were left over. You can put them in the picture anywhere you want. They're easy to draw, see?

What's the Big Idea?

Jesus taught an important lesson that day. If we give God our best and trust Him, He will always take what we've given Him and make it so much more than we could ever imagine.

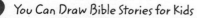

16

Zaccheus up a Tree
Luke 19:1–10

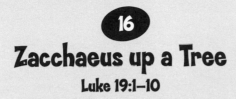

Zacchaeus. . .quick, come down! I must be a guest in your home today.
—LUKE 19:5

Wherever Jesus went, huge crowds of people followed. As He entered the gates of Jericho one day, the mob was so big that He could barely get through. This huge crowd created a problem for one guy who lived in the little town. He was really rich, really unpopular, and really short. His name was Zacchaeus.

Draw some money bags and gold all around Zacchaeus. He might not have had any friends, but he sure was rich.

Zacchaeus was a dishonest tax collector, and that made him very unpopular with the residents of Jericho. None of them wanted to help him squeeze through the crowd to see Jesus.

But nobody ever said Zacchaeus was dumb (that we know of). He knew of a big sycamore tree about a block away, right where Jesus would pass by.

Perfect! Zach thought as he jogged down the street ahead of the crowd. When he reached the tree, he hiked up his robe and climbed up limb by limb. Once he found a suitable branch, he sat down, got comfortable, and waited to see the man he'd heard so much about. Finally Jesus appeared around a corner.

Draw what you think Zacchaeus looked like up in the big tree. Begin with three little rocks. The big middle rock is going to be Zach's head. So draw his eyes, his nose, and a circle for his beard. Now fill in his beard and make his mouth and his little cap.

Since he's up in the tree, he's got to hang on, so make his hands like this. And add his feet just dangling there while he climbs. Hang on, Zach!

Do you like to climb trees?

*H*a! Now I'm going to see this guy for myself, Zacchaeus thought. *There He is! Wow, He looks cool. And the people seem to really love Him.*

Zacchaeus didn't know what that felt like.

Then something strange happened. Just as Jesus reached the spot where Zacchaeus was, He stopped, looked right up at the little tax collector in the tree, and said, "Hey, Zacchaeus, come on down—I want to stay at your house!"

Draw the sycamore tree around Zach. You can just make a big circle or draw in some leaves and branches.

Well, Zacchaeus was so surprised that he almost fell out of the tree! He scurried down, ran to his house, and welcomed Jesus, His disciples, and a whole bunch of His friends to a banquet.

After the meal was over, Zacchaeus stood up and addressed the crowd.

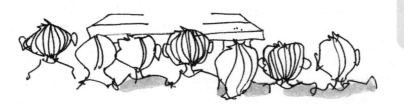

Draw Zach on the tabletop speaking to the crowd. Draw Jesus next to him.

"Jesus, just being with You has changed my life. I'm not going to cheat anybody anymore, and whatever I've stolen, I'm going to pay back four times as much!"

Jesus smiled. "Welcome to the family," He said.

What's the Big Idea?

Why do you suppose Jesus stopped and spent the day with Zacchaeus, of all people? After all, he was selfish, rude, and unpopular. Or is that the *reason* Jesus did it? Aren't you glad we don't have to be popular or talented for God to love us? He loves us just the way we are!

Palm Sunday
Matthew 21:1–11

Most of the crowd spread their garments on the road ahead of him, and others cut branches from the trees and spread them on the road.
—MATTHEW 21:8

I want you to do Me a favor," Jesus said to two of His disciples. "Go into the village and get something for Me."

"Sure, Jesus. Anything."

"As soon as you get to town, you'll see a little donkey colt tied up. Just untie him and bring him here to Me."

Jesus must have known what they were thinking because He added, "If anyone asks you what you're doing, just say that the Lord needs him."

The disciples did just as they were told and brought the donkey to Jesus.

"Here he is. Nobody's ever ridden on him before," they said.

"Perfect."

The disciples put some of their garments on the back of the colt for Jesus to sit on.

What happened next was a huge surprise for the disciples. As Jesus calmly rode the donkey up the hill to Jerusalem, people seemed to appear out of nowhere, holding palm branches, laying their clothes on the road in front of Jesus, and shouting, "Hosanna! Blessed is He who comes in the name of the Lord!"

Draw the palm branches the people are holding. Here's a tip on how to draw them. Start with a straight line. Now add the leaves, starting with bigger ones near the bottom and making them smaller as they reach the top.

Try drawing some more people with palm branches in this picture.

"They're treating Jesus like a king," one of the disciples noted. "The palm branches, the clothes…" He knew this was how people welcomed visiting royalty into the city. The crowd swarmed all around Jesus as He reached the gate.

The prophet Zechariah had predicted this triumphal entry into the city more than 450 years earlier. "Rejoice, O people of Zion! Shout in triumph, O people of Jerusalem! Look, your king is coming to you. He is righteous and victorious, yet he is humble, riding on a donkey—riding on a donkey's colt" (Zechariah 9:9).

Yes, Jesus really was the Messiah, the One sent to save the people, but God's plan was a lot different from what they were expecting!

Let's draw the donkey. Here's a sample.

Start with an upside down *L*. That's the donkey's head. And of course they have long ears, so add those now (but not *too* long). Now draw two eyes and the donkey's nose, and start the body like this. This might require some practice. Complete the oval for the donkey's body and add the legs. Now see if you can draw the donkey in this picture so it looks like Jesus is riding it. Very good!

Here's Jesus riding the donkey into Jerusalem. Draw all the people welcoming Him, shouting, and waving palm branches.

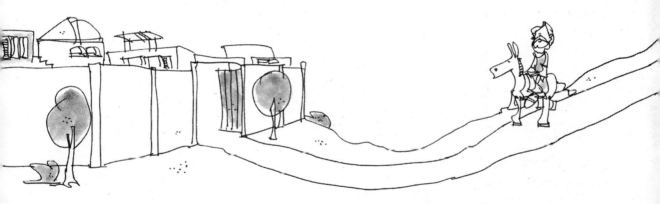

"HOSANNA" means "Save us—now!"

The people thought Jesus was going be their Ruler. They wanted Him to kick the Romans out of Israel and save the people from Rome's mean and unjust ways.

What's the Big Idea?

Imagine the dramatic and exciting scene of Jesus riding into Jerusalem. Some people were waving palm branches, and kids were shouting and praising. They were welcoming a King! Only Jesus knew that He was being sent to the city for a different reason. He came to give His life so that all of us could begin a friendship with God.

18

He Is Risen!
Luke 24:1–12

Why are you looking among the dead for someone who is alive? He isn't here! He is risen from the dead!
—LUKE 24:5-6

Jesus had ridden the donkey into Jerusalem on a Sunday. On the following Friday, the Jewish leaders turned the people against Jesus, and they convinced the Romans to crucify Him. Soldiers nailed Him to a cross, where He hung for hours until He died. He knew this was why He had come—to die in our place and take the punishment for all our sins. Because of what He did that dark, lonely Friday afternoon, we now can come to God and be His kids.

But Friday isn't the end of the story. On Sunday morning, Jesus rose from the dead, came out of the tomb, and greeted His friends.

Can you imagine how amazing that must have been? Now we can live forever with Him because of what He did—He opened the way for us.

An angel gave the disciples the good news about Jesus. He was sitting on the stone that had been in front of the tomb.

Let's try drawing a picture of the angel who greeted the disciples. We'll start with a shape that looks like a house with a chimney coming out of it. That's going to be his robe. Add some fingers and his head (just a circle will do). Now draw a nice excited face on your angel and add ears and some hair. Draw his belt, his feet, and of course his wings! He's got some pretty great news!

Draw the angel

Matthew 28:2 says the angel was sitting on the round stone that had been in front of the tomb. In this picture we've got the tomb and the angel, but can you draw the stone and his wings?

Here's a hillside and the empty tomb. Jesus was crucified between two criminals, so draw three crosses on top of the hill. And draw some more trees and bushes down by the opening because John 19:41 says that Jesus' tomb was in a garden.

Draw a picture of what you think heaven is like.

What's the Big Idea?

Jesus came to take our place and suffer the punishment for our sins. He did that on the cross. But then on the third day, He rose from the dead! He beat the grave! This is His promise to us—if we put our trust in Him and follow Him, we'll live forever with Him in heaven.

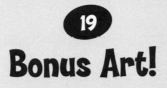

19

Bonus Art!

Draw close to God, and God will draw close to you.
—James 4:8 (NKJV)

Hold on to your hat! You've just crossed into the bonus section of this book. We're going to learn how to draw a couple things that weren't mentioned in the stories so far.

Roman Soldier

The first is a Roman soldier about the time when Jesus walked the earth. These guys are fun to draw.

Draw the beginnings of a house. Don't complete the roof. Add a triangle on the top and another on the side. These are parts of his helmet. Add a couple of lines for his eyebrows and mouth.

Now draw a semicircle on top. Add the brush thing that goes on the helmet.

If you'd like, draw some of his body. Roman soldiers wore breastplates made out of bronze that protected them in battle. Sometimes they wore capes too. They'd use these capes as blankets if they had to sleep outside.

You can also give him a spear and a sword. The sword was short, about 18 inches long, and useful for close fighting. Or for slicing a pastrami sandwich.

Draw the Roman Soldier

Home Sweet Home

People lived pretty simply during Jesus' time. Their houses were small, square, and usually just had one room for eating, sleeping, and hanging out. Sometimes even the sheep and goats stayed in the house with the family. Let's try drawing a square house.

You can make it 3-D by adding the side and roof.

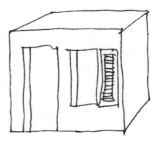

Get a Haircut

In Bible times, most men had beards and mustaches.

Add some beards, mustaches, and goatees to these faces. You might even add some long hair on a couple of these guys or make them bald. Do you remember which Old Testament prophet was called "baldy"?

You Can Draw Bible Stories for Kids